CONFIDENCE

IN 40 IMAGES

Published in 2023 by The School of Life
First published in the USA in 2023
930 High Road, London, N12 9RT

Copyright © The School of Life 2023

Designed and typeset by Marcia Mihotich
Printed in Slovenia by DZS Grafik

A proportion of this book has appeared online at
www.theschooloflife.com/articles

Every effort has been made to contact the copyright holders
of the material reproduced in this book. If any have been
inadvertently overlooked, the publisher will be pleased to make
restitution at the earliest opportunity.

The School of Life publishes a range of books on essential topics
in psychological and emotional life, including relationships,
parenting, friendship, careers and fulfilment. The aim is always
to help us to understand ourselves better – and thereby to grow
calmer, less confused and more purposeful. Discover our full
range of titles, including books for children, here:
www.theschooloflife.com/books

The School of Life also offers a comprehensive therapy service,
which complements, and draws upon, our published works:
www.theschooloflife.com/therapy

www.theschooloflife.com

ISBN 978-1-915087-30-0

10 9 8 7 6 5 4 3 2 1

MIX
Paper | Supporting
responsible forestry
FSC® C106600
FSC
www.fsc.org

CONFIDENCE
IN 40 IMAGES

The School of Life

CONTENTS

INTRODUCTION

It would be comforting to believe that the difference between success and failure could be attributed to intelligence, hard work or, perhaps, some form of divine favour. After all, these are things that the world has thought a lot about – and can offer sophisticated help with; there are schools that train our brains for exams, businesses that exhort us to improve on our annual targets, and all manner of churches, shrines and temples that guarantee us rewards from heavenly spirits in return for prayers.

Yet the route to genuine success seems more elusive, uncharted and complicated than these methods imply. There are dauntingly clever people who never seem to make the kind of progress that their IQs would predict. There are workers who rise before dawn and toil till midnight and yet have little to show for their exertions after a life-time of labour. Intense prayer is especially unpredictable in its results.

In reality, what often determines the difference between success and failure is a quality that isn't generally taught in any mainstream school or college, that businesses maintain a confused or embarrassed silence about and that religions tend to view as contrary to the tenor of their teachings – namely, confidence. When ascertaining why one person has been able to drive their ideas forward, overcome inhibitions, withstand opposition and hold on to their distinctive vision, while another has languished, gone with the crowd, buckled or sacrificed their truths, it is almost always an issue of confidence that is at play.

Confidence means the ability to meet the world substantially on our terms, not to be afraid of our own voice or embarrassed by our wishes and ideas – and an inner resourcefulness to withstand criticism and mockery for the sake of what we hold to be important.

It can seem as if a person's degree of confidence must simply be a matter of chance, a gift from above or a freakish genetic inheritance – not something that could systematically be investigated or altered. But the truth is a good deal more flexible and hopeful. There is no such thing as inborn confidence and therefore no a priori block to bolstering our levels of it. We can, with the right tools, grow more confident in the same way we can become more proficient in a language or adept at a sport. Confidence is teachable; we do not have to retain the meek and self-suspicious natures we may currently be burdened with.

There is a further claim: one of the ways in which confidence can be acquired is via looking at the right sort of images. Just as many of these can be held responsible for sapping our spirits and destroying our levels of self-belief, so too a curation of an optimal gallery can help to restore our levels of tenacity and bolster our reserves of self-esteem.

What follows is a tour around a small imaginary museum dedicated to one of the most powerful capacities underpinning our chances of fulfilment and joy.

In an adolescent's bedroom, devoid of any of the grandeur or aesthetic sophistication of a museum, we have a chance to observe with particular clarity a question that art critics and theoreticians tend to tiptoe around with fateful squeamishness: what is the point of art?

The answer from Georgina's bedroom is clear: the point of art is to lend us the courage to become who we really are. Art is there so that we can look up in the morning – confused and apprehensive about the day ahead – and quickly rediscover, in compressed visual form, reminders of what we value, whom we admire and what we are aiming to be. Art functions as a stable repository of our intermittently unsteady but essential selves.

There is much that matters intensely to Georgina. She cares about the mental stamina and physical prowess of athletes; she cares about the lyrics of singers who know about her pain and have answers to its sources; and she cares about the beauty of men whom she longs to be with yet is, for now, too shy to talk to. But, away from her bedroom, Georgina's identity is not so resolute. In certain moods, she might think those athletes don't matter so much really; maybe the perspectives of her favourite singers don't hold water; or perhaps those men will always be out of reach. However, with the help of her bedroom, Georgina can recover her strength. She has created a shrine to her ideals and is asking her icons to help her rehearse her faith in herself.

We might not share Georgina's particular aesthetic or values, but her underlying move is universal. We, too, need to create a den or private museum and fill it with works that can beam back to us, in our wavering moments, a picture of whom we want to be and what our lives should be dedicated to. We, too, need to become skilful curators of those images that can help us to keep our true selves in view.

Rania Matar, *Georgina, Roxbury, Massachusetts*, 2010

One reason why we may withdraw from the entire idea of becoming more confident is the images we carry in our minds about what a confident person might be like. Confidence can seem synonymous with brash arrogance and unthinking boosterism; with the chiselled-jaw sports captain we knew from university or the garrulous financier we met on holiday. We can end up taking counterproductive pride in underselling ourselves and staying quiet because we cannot find any confident characters with whom we would remotely seek to identify.

Hence the importance of a group of people sitting on a lawn in a square in central London in 1915. They belonged to what we now know as the Bloomsbury Group, the most influential intellectual movement of its age, responsible for pioneering developments in literature, science, economics and art. Part of what distinguished these avant-garde thinkers was the extremely cautious and outwardly modest way in which they carried out their revolution. Many were known for their manners and their shyness: the painter and costume designer Duncan Grant mumbled 'sorry' whenever he could; the biographer Lytton Strachey (with the beard) spoke in a low, respectful mumble; and the artist Vanessa Bell tended always to ask others questions to downplay her own intelligence.

Nevertheless, these men and women took a sledge-hammer to the stifling verities of the Victorian age and ushered in the modern world: the economist John Maynard Keynes invented the welfare state; Virginia Woolf remade the novel; Vanessa Bell introduced abstraction into British art. But they did so with confidence of a particular sort; a kind compatible with politeness, humility, smiles – and tea.

We may be in danger of gravely neglecting our potential so long as we continue to operate with a brittle concept of what confidence might look like. We can, in reality, be quiet and confident, gentle and confident, thoughtful and confident. We can remain ourselves even as we adopt an underlying steeliness that infuses our projects with power and our thoughts with resolve. We can change the world without having to be bullies – or losing our manners.

Members of the Bloomsbury Group, a London garden, 1915 (left to right: Lady Ottoline Morrell, Maria Nys, Lytton Strachey, Duncan Grant and Vanessa Bell)

In mid-September 1888, a penniless Dutchman, who would be committed to an asylum in a few months and be dead within two years, sat down in the eastern corner of the Place du Forum in Arles, France and set to work on one of the most astonishing and beloved paintings ever made. *Café Terrace at Night* juxtaposes our snug night-time rituals under our defiant artificial lamps with the ultimate mysteries and sublimity of the cosmos.

And yet, as we know, van Gogh found no buyers for his masterpiece; no museum came begging, no gallery gave a damn. His work appeared wholly worthless to his entire era. He could barely afford lunch or a new pair of shoes. The local children mocked him. Rarely has a more despised or marginal figure walked the earth. The story is so familiar that we are apt to lose sight of its ongoing relevance and universal import: people miss things ... on a very large scale. They did so then – and, by implication, they must continue to do so now. The reasons are not very complicated and don't belong to any sort of conspiracy; essentially, humans are herd animals. They show immense loyalty to groupthink and resolute opposition to independent analysis. They follow what is fashionable. They are appalled where they are told to be appalled – and admiring where they are told to admire. They will bow to van Gogh when instructed to and stamp on him when no one tells them not to.

Without making any claims for our genius, we should take inspiration from this. If there are ways in which we are presently neglected and criticised, we should be wholly unsurprised and, more importantly, unfrightened. This is the way things have always been and will always be.

An alternative to hating and undermining ourselves is to be, at points, a lot more particular about the sort of people we live among.

Vincent van Gogh, *Café Terrace at Night*, 1888

The British photographer Martin Parr has spent the better part of his career photographing people at the beach in distinctive poses. His bodies typically appear vast, distended, sunburnt, hairy and wrinkled. His people are stuffing themselves with fried chicken or glutinous pastries, they're reading tawdry newspapers and the kids are smeared with ice cream, while, in their tight underpants or stretched floral bikinis, their parents look dazed, selfish and not a little stupid.

This is no place to adjudicate on the degrees of meanness or patronisation at play; what we can acknowledge is how useful Parr's photographs are as a means of shaking us from certain undeserved forms of underconfidence.

We too often step back from pursuing our agenda because of a dread of how 'other people' might respond. We worry what they might say about our creative projects, our designs for our careers or our way of arranging our personal lives. We are rendered meek by the intensity of our respect for strangers.

But, under Parr's guidance, we can dare to think that we have perhaps not been forensic enough in assessing who 'other people' really are. We may have imputed elevated degrees of intelligence, wisdom and goodness where these don't belong – and suffered as a result.

Our kindness and respect mean that we may have given the advantage to the crowd while downplaying the merits of our own vision. We may need to grow systematically rude about strangers and insist on the prevalence of idiocy and thoughtlessness – at the beach and, by extension, across whole landmasses – in order that we can be appropriately respectful of our own ideas and plans.

The framing of those sunburnt bodies may not be very generous, but it can liberate us from a fruitless and unnecessary modesty of mind. We will not be able to get on and do what we think is right until we have properly taken on board how unimpressive and uncaring a vast majority of our fellow citizens might really be.

Martin Parr, *Beach Therapy*, 2018

The American writer James Baldwin first went to Paris in 1948 as a 24-year-old, and he was to stay in the city for much of the next nine years – and in France intermittently until his death in 1987.

Baldwin had felt asphyxiated in America: his family had expectations of him that he hated, his friends were judgemental and he felt observed and intruded upon. Society was moralistic and prurient. As a result, he couldn't be creative or free, and he had the sense of being watched and commented upon all the time; it was like being always at school – or in prison.

So he undertook that most inwardly liberating of moves: he went into exile. From Paris, it no longer mattered what 'they' were saying. Public opinion could appear, as it always should have done, parochial and absurd. No one knew him in the French capital. They had never heard of his family. It was as if he had – in a good way – died and been granted a chance at a second, unsigned life. In France, he could create, take risks, dress differently, make unusual friends ... and become himself.

Crucially, Baldwin had no interest whatsoever in assimilating into French society. He wasn't looking to swap one narrow village for another. It was exile he was after – that very particular state in which one is free not to belong anywhere in particular, to escape all tribes in order to be unobserved, anonymous and detached.

It may not always be possible for us to become actual exiles, but we should at the very least strive to become internal exiles; that is, people who can behave like visitors in their own lands, no longer bound by local idiosyncrasies, able to cut themselves off from the mean and restricted views of so-called friends or disloyal families, and to grow indifferent to provincial competition and grandstanding.

Baldwin and his fellow exiles are there to teach us about what freedom might feel like. We should strive to follow them in our minds and, one day perhaps, in our actual living arrangements.

Sophie Bassouls, *James Baldwin on the Quai des Grands Augustins, Paris*, April 1972

One of the reasons why we are less confident than we might be is because of a fundamental difference between what we know of ourselves and what we know of other people – especially impressive, grand, enviable people whom we might wish to emulate or learn from.

We know so much about our own hesitation, our shyness, our clumsiness and our insecurity. We are desperately aware of how lazy we are, how sentimental, how vain and how absurd. We have intimate knowledge of our disgusting bodily habits and revolting moral weaknesses. We know about all sorts of embarrassing things we have done: messages we sent, advances we made, gauche sentences we uttered.

And yet of those enviable, distant others we know – comparatively – so very little. We have no evidence that they ever woke up in the middle of the night sobbing at their own stupidity or repulsiveness. We don't know how anxious they are in meetings. We can't tell what levels of despair they experience at the start of a new week. We don't know how silly and child-like they can be. We know them only from the carefully edited self-portraits they put out into the world.

Out of ignorance and undue self-suspicion, we therefore discount ourselves as plausible players from the start.

Surely no one who farts as we do has ever made it to high places; surely no one as needy as we are has ever won esteem.

Certain legendary figures are kind in letting us see some of the reality behind the mask and, perhaps while holding a baby aloft, hinting at more human, unguarded and vulnerable dimensions. But where we have no such information, we should imagine what we haven't been shown. We need to recall at all times the structural imbalance between what we see of ourselves and what we know of those we admire. We aren't necessarily so inept or so ignorant: we just know a lot more about us and a lot less about them. We should dare to try; everyone is to be found on the toilet at least once a day.

Pete Souza, *US President Obama and Ella Rhodes, daughter of Deputy National Security Advisor Ben Rhodes, White House*, October 2015

It's an inevitable feature of the way in which the world is structured that, without quite noticing, we are principally exposed to the finished products of others. In restaurants, we are served cooked meals rather than raw ingredients. At comedy shows, we hear polished jokes, not stumbling first goes. At airports, we board certified airliners, not utopian prototypes. And in bookshops, we are offered texts that have undergone repeated cycles of editing and rewriting.

The problem for our confidence is that, while we are exposed to the flawless output of others, we know our own work only from its roughest, most dispiriting and most frightening early attempts. Who would not lose courage on standing back from their first moves at writing a book? Who would not recoil at their fledging beginnings in art, cookery, aeronautics, public speaking, parenting, judo – or pretty much any activity at which humans can eventually excel?

Marcel Proust began writing the greatest novel in the French language in his bedroom in central Paris in the summer of 1908; he was 37 years old and had been unsuccessfully trying to become a writer since his late teens. He had put aside three previous novels, had been rejected by every prestigious publishing house and had never earned any money from his pen. At first, the new novel didn't seem any more promising: the early drafts were a chaos of crossings out and tentative scribbles. But Proust did not lose courage. He had mastered the central principle of productive outcomes: the art of keeping going.

As readers, we can feel grateful that Proust eventually worked up his scribbles into flawless paragraphs; as writers, we would be wise to notice for just how long things remained an alarming mess. Like almost everything worth doing, literature rewards momentous patience and ceaseless incremental toil. We should forgive ourselves the horror of our first drafts – and pointedly seek out the first drafts of those we most admire.

Marcel Proust, manuscript pages, *In Search of Lost Time*, 1909

It's a pity – as far as our collective levels of confidence are concerned – that more visitors to Paris don't end up in the solemn and unshowy galleries of the Musée des Arts et Métiers, an institution dedicated to displaying the history of scientific and technological instruments. Rows upon rows of cabinets show the development of all manner of gadgets that we either ignore or take for granted in their modern forms. We see the evolution of waterwheels, telephones, radiographs, telescopes, electrical switchboards, undersea cables, pneumatic tyres, aerials, calculators ...

What is moving is the implicit patience on display. It cannot have been easy, at the dawn of the invention of photography, to feel the full promise of the technology and yet to know that, given the state of material science and the slow pace of iterative progress, one would almost certainly be dead before a properly sharp and colourful image could ever come to light.

Humans had been trying to capture reality and replay it faithfully back to themselves for a thousand years when Auguste and Louis Lumière cobbled together their pioneering cinematograph, which housed – within a massive clunky metal casing – a magic lantern lamp house,

a camera, a projector and a printer. Numerous times the machine overheated, the film reel dangled precipitously between the main projector box and an external spool and, when it eventually worked – at the world's first cinema show at the Grand Café on the Boulevard des Capucines in Paris in December 1895 – the machine let out what was at best a flickering, indecipherable grey-black gribouillage.

Still, the Lumière brothers did not despair and neither did the thousands of engineers who came in their wake. They contented themselves with making one small innovation at a time. They did not mind leaving glory to future generations. One comically large and heavy box followed another. What today fits in our pockets used to require a barn. All of us are, in different ways, working on prototypes. Those who succeed don't panic at the thought that they might not be around to see the fruition of their ideas; they know we are all condemned to die midchapter. They're just pleased to be somewhere on the right path towards something worthwhile.

Lumière Cinematograph, 1895

There is particular confidence to be gained from careful study of the subsection of celebrity photography that features people of achievement or distinction long before they acquired the credentials we came to know them for. There they are in grainy pictures, at the supermarket or on the university steps, with buck teeth or acne, hesitant smiles or ill-fitting clothes. We recognise them at once, but it takes a moment to trace exactly what changed across the decades.

There is implicit encouragement in their tentative eyes because they managed to surmount so much. For a start, the physical side of things: they learnt how to dress, they outgrew their wispy hair, they sorted out their skin. But, at a deeper level, they mastered their self-doubt. They came to terms with their flaws and the voices inside their heads that must have told them – as do ours – that they weren't good enough and that they couldn't do it. No doubt some of those voices didn't disappear entirely. They probably still resonate in some part of their minds today, but these people acquired the knack of not heeding the call to back down. They refused to spend the rest of their lives apologising for who they were.

Their examples are open for us to follow. We perhaps look much more like their young selves than we do their mature ones – or at least that's what we feel like. Yet the path from gauche novice to accomplished artist, politician, businessperson or scientist does not have to be inherently mysterious or barred. Ordinary boys and girls in bad jeans have made it – and we might too.

We don't have to hate ourselves for our current imperfections. Of course we are less than impressive right now, but there is time to take things in hand. If we can't overcome our shame at who we are, we will never have anything we can one day look back on and be proud of. If we are not embarrassed by who we were last year, we are not learning enough.

Tony Blair, St John's College, Oxford, 1972

We are, with great skill, being invited to have a good laugh at deference. In a grand English country house, the photographer Bill Brandt has captured an attitude of acute class consciousness and inhibition. A parlourmaid, who has devoted her life to what she would have called her 'betters', looks on with intense seriousness at the table she oversees. Her younger colleague looks less stern, but equally cowed and awed. Yet we know that their careful handiwork will be of no concern whatsoever to the braying band of upper-class dolts with names like Rupert and Jemima who are about to burst in for dinner.

We may feel relief – and implicit superiority – on noticing the date of the picture. How silly they were back then; how free and modern we are today. But before celebrating our enlightenment, we should pause to acknowledge a darker possibility: we are the descendants of people who spent the better part of the last 200,000 years serving their masters and mistresses. It is only in the last second of historical evolution that we have finally tasted democracy and a spirit of equality.

It is, therefore, hugely unlikely that we have in one bound entirely thrown off the legacy of feudalism. We are perhaps no longer officially in bondage, but the attitudes that came with servitude almost certainly continue to temper our aspirations and structure our hopes. Few of us are now formally servants; fewer of us still know how to be free. Without our noticing, we are likely to operate with the self-limiting beliefs of the past. We are serfs in the lack of imagination that we bring to our work, in our timidity of thought and in our submission to the sadistic agendas of others. Our sense of inferiority has a surprisingly long after-life – and never more so than when we believe it to be over.

True liberation begins with greater pessimism – by accepting the extent to which we may, at critical junctures, remain under-parlourmaids of the mind.

Bill Brandt, *Parlourmaid and Under-Parlourmaid Ready to Serve Dinner*, 1938

We may not know his identity precisely, but we recognise the type well enough from the annals of European art: an aristocratic young man, full of the sense of pride and haughtiness of his class, gazes down at us commoners with disdain and indifference. There might be an ancient castle to inherit, a very long and complicated title to his name, a coat of arms and skill at archery and fencing.

It is easy to mock, but more interesting to dare to admire. What stands out is how little this young man cares about what we think. He holds none of the illusions of democracy. He doesn't believe the crowd has anything to teach him. He places no faith in the opinions of the majority. He has never harboured hopes of public recognition or longed-for acclaim from the masses. He knows that idiocy is rife and vulgarity everywhere. He can trust that elevated people are in a sharp minority. He doesn't need you to like him. And therefore he is free.

We might protest that we could not possibly emulate such attitudes: we have no castle, we can't trace our ancestors back to Charlemagne, we are democrats ... Nevertheless, we limit the concept of aristocracy unhelpfully when we associate it simply with a restricted franchise and country houses. We may be able to become something far more relevant and more flexible than an aristocrat of the blood: an aristocrat of the spirit.

By this, one means someone who, while they might not be living in a fancy house, does not automatically assent to the majority view; someone who operates with their own value system in which pride of place is given to kindness, thoughtfulness and sensitivity. Such aristocrats will not rage or cheer when they are commanded to. They are those rare beings: elitists of the heart.

It is not always easy to live in mass democracies. Without having any interest in changing the voting system, aristocrats of the spirit can embolden us to refuse the tyranny of the majority.

Bronzino, *Portrait of a Young Man*, 1530s

There have been few writers as brave as Victor Hugo. Over a turbulent sixty-year career, he fought fiercely for what he believed in: republican government, medieval architecture, an end to capital punishment, school and prison reform, a United States of Europe and the right to lead the kind of complicated private life that upsets prudes. We shouldn't allow his posthumous acclaim to disguise how much he was, in certain quarters, loathed in his lifetime.

And yet, as his portrait suggests, he knew full well how to face down critics. In 1845, Hugo's friend, the academic and politician Abel-François Villemain, fell into despair because of rumours about his sexuality and attacks on his work by professional enemies. Only concern for his daughters prevented Villemain from killing himself. Fortunately, Hugo was both a good friend and a great consoler – and he came over one evening to shake Villemain from his sorrow:

'You have enemies! Well, who doesn't have them? Guizot has enemies, Thiers has enemies, Lamartine has enemies. Haven't I myself been fighting for twenty years? Haven't I spent twenty years being hated, sold down the river, betrayed, reviled, taunted and insulted? Have my books not been ridiculed and my actions travestied? I've had traps set for me; I've even fallen into a few ... What do I care? I have contempt. It's one of the hardest but also most necessary things in life to learn to have contempt. Contempt protects and crushes. It's like a breastplate and an axe. Do you have enemies? That's simply the fate of anyone who has done anything worthwhile or launched any new idea. It's a necessary fog that clings to anything that shines. Fame must have enemies, as light must have gnats. Don't worry about it; just have contempt. Keep your spirit serene and your life lucid. Never give your enemies the satisfaction of thinking that they've been able to cause you grief or pain. Stay happy, cheerful, contemptuous and firm.'

People-pleasing carries grave risks, as Hugo knew only too well – it's contempt that can save our lives.

Étienne Carjat, *Victor Hugo*, 1876

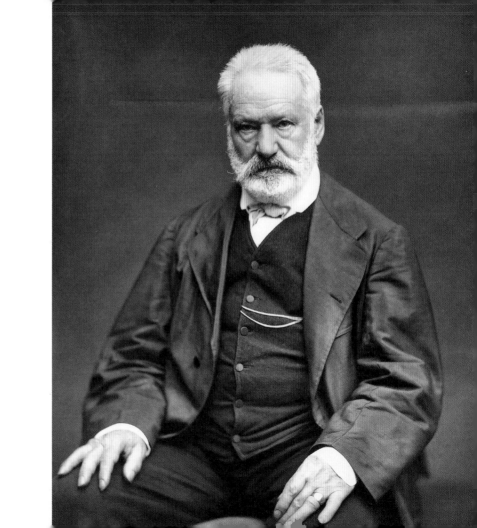

Why do people's levels of confidence differ so much? Why does one person feel free to dress how they please, to follow their professional dreams and to pursue their own sexual tastes, while another spends their entire life in timidity, resignation and compliance?

We can venture: confidence is the fruit of having been boundlessly and extravagantly loved by an adult in the early years. The strength to withstand attack, ignore critics and fight back against one's enemies is – almost always – the beautiful, fortunate fruit of having felt indomitably at the centre of someone else's affection for as long as it took for our bones to harden and our spirits to rise.

Confidence-inducing behaviour has little of the robustness of confidence itself. Its hallmark is tenderness. It starts with someone being profoundly pleased to see us when they pull back the curtains in the morning. We are their champion, their tiny button and their adored little rabbit. They love our limbs and our cheeks, our hair and our toes. When we are sick, they stay with us through the night. When we show them a drawing, they consider it with huge care. They hold our hand as we go to the park. They put cream on our blisters. They tell us not to listen to bullies. They make us feel at the centre of the universe.

Thereafter, it simply doesn't matter quite so much if the whole world decides it hates us. The love of millions won't compensate for the absence of such love, and its presence will fortify us against all manner of opprobrium.

We can't go back and magically refind this emotional nectar, but it pays to know what we were deprived of and what hole we may therefore still have to fill. And if we feel solid in ourselves, we should be careful never to forget that there is a someone, most probably a 'she', in whose inordinate debt we are – and whom we might want to call soon to say thank you for our sanity.

Mary Cassatt, *Mother and Child*, 1914

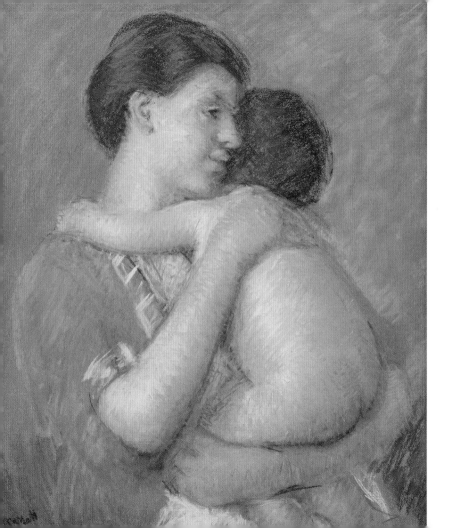

35

Despite so much talk of love, it can be easy to forget what the point of relationships really is. It isn't, in the end, a matter of sex (however nice that is) or shared intellectual tastes or mutual enthusiasms for sport or travel. It is, strangely but crucially, about the gifting of confidence. Love is a privileged arena in which two people can lend one another the confidence to endure the ongoing stresses, regrets and sorrows of existence.

We tend to miss the point because those who enjoy such love don't often reveal their privilege. When we see a grown-up acting with defiance and strength – hosting conferences, taking over companies, running countries – there is almost always a person (they might be, for example, a quiet quantum chemist) in the background ensuring the success of the performance. The world may know the heroic figure as the chancellor, the president or the professor, but, in the sustaining arms of their companion, they are simply 'tiny one', 'gagou' or 'baby'. Every fear that 'baby' has can be shared – often in the middle of the night – and reframed by their partner in a less catastrophic light. Solutions small and large can be found: where to leave the umbrella, how many pills to take, what to do with the money … The caring partner knows about the issues with digestion and when there might be a need for a toilet. We need to be cared for like helpless infants in the night to be strong enough for the adult roles expected of us in the day.

We easily lose our priorities when we anticipate relationships. There is ultimately only one issue that should concern us on an early dinner date. They may be beautiful, witty, athletic and well-read, but that is all by the by compared to the truly crucial theme at stake: *Is this someone who could give me confidence? Could they soothe me?* And, most centrally of all: *Might I sometimes be 'baby' with them … ?*

Chancellor Angela Merkel of Germany with her husband, Joachim Sauer, 2013

On the tiny island of Santa Ana in the Solomon Islands, young men have traditionally devoted their lives to the hunting of a tuna-like fish called the bonito. Catching bonitos isn't easy – they are fast swimmers, they attract sharks in their wake and the Pacific is filled with treacherous currents. There are moments in young fishermen's lives when they must doubt whether they will ever make it home.

To lend them confidence, novices are invited to take part in an initiation ceremony. In a special hall, they stand beneath a gigantic carved wooden bonito, inside of which a skull has been placed belonging to one of the community's most revered elder fishermen. The symbolic presence of a wise and experienced ancestor at the heart of the bonito is intended to fill onlookers with courage and hope. When the men are out at sea and the swell starts to build, they will better be able to imagine what an ancestor might have said to reassure them; they might grow a little more certain that they, too, might reach a ripe old age and that the bonito might be theirs after an exhausting struggle.

We may not ourselves be hunting any ray-finned fish off the coast of a Pacific island, but the bonito reliquary provides us with a universally valid metaphor for what becoming confident involves. We need to develop faith in ourselves by internalising the voices of those who have mastered challenges before us. We need to swallow our kindest forebears so that when we are next out on the 'high seas' there can be a calming voice inside us telling us not to give up and not to be scared. However, rather than this being the voice of a Melanesian chief, it might belong to Marcus Aurelius, our older sister or a perceptive psychotherapist.

We have voices in our minds already. They often say the nastiest things: 'I knew you couldn't do it', 'You're pathetic ...' We should follow the inhabitants of the Solomon Islands in making sure the process of swallowing people is conscious and focused on internalising only the kindest and shrewdest voices available.

Bonito tuna, reliquary fish, Santa Ana, Solomon Islands, early 20th century

For many hundreds of years, all over the world, millions of people have gathered at the feet of a person we might as well call 'Mummy' and shared their sorrows, admitted their sins and confusions and collapsed in tears. To make things psychologically more acceptable, denominations have been clever enough to call this mummy 'the Virgin Mary' and wrapped up her identity in a Biblical story about Jesus and the redemption of humanity. But nothing quite obscures the fact that the Virgin Mary, insofar as she delivers solace, does so principally because she skilfully reactivates semi-conscious memories of the kindly female caregivers of our early years.

It doesn't quite matter what has knocked our confidence: perhaps we have been attacked by people at work, maybe our relationship is no longer working or we might be exhausted by our families. Mary's beseeching, warm eyes – evocatively rendered by artists across the ages – welcome us in our distress. Mary doesn't judge or harangue; she merely wants to gift us her infinite compassion – of course it has been hard; how could we have known; poor us ...

Atheists have focused immense energy on the question of whether or not religion is 'true'. What surely matters more is how useful it can be – and how badly we might require the Marian consolation some branches of it offer. It tells us something key that whole cathedrals have been built in the Virgin's name. Religions have the true measure of our dependent needs. Were we to be tasked with the project of inventing a new religion, we would be wise to ensure that a Mary-like figure – kindly, comforting and sympathetic – was close to its centre. We may not presently worship a 'mummy' ourselves, but such outward reserve should only make us wonder how and where we are managing to address the vulnerable needs she embodies and that none of us can – or should – ever fully outgrow.

Diana Markosian, *Worshippers pray to the Virgin Mary in the village of Medjugorje, Bosnia and Herzegovina*, 2015

When we think of what a good parent might be like, we rarely imagine someone who would sit blithely by while their small child did a handstand in a restaurant – especially when their dinner had just been put in front of them and Granny might be at the table too. Or someone who would let their child call the headteacher a 'fat poo' or, a few years later, would let their teenager scream at them that they never asked to be born.

We associate decent childhoods with polite, well-behaved offspring who know how to defer, to keep a lid on their feelings and to smile in front of strangers.

But there is a paradox: the more we ask a child to be 'good', the more the life we are ultimately setting them up for may be hemmed in by counterproductive degrees of compromise and renunciation. We know how to worry a lot about 'bad' children – the sort who graffiti the underpass and start drinking too young – but we know far less about the problems engendered by so-called good children, those who are overly adept at meeting the expectations of others while being scared of exploring their own potential. These are the children of people too depressed, furious or neglectful to allow their offspring to give rebellion a go – and to develop the confidence to push back against the wishes of others.

To equip a child for the adult world doesn't simply mean training them in abnegation and sacrifice. It doesn't mean bringing up people-pleasers. It means paving the way for children who have the inner strength to say no to those who seek to bully them, and who feel loved enough in their core to withstand opposition and rejection. And that, in turn, may mean allowing small children the necessary margin to pull off the odd tantrum and finish their gymnastics before dinner; these may be the unusual preconditions for eventual adult lives worth living.

Andy Bishop, *Lively child and exasperated mother*, date unknown

There are periods in life in which it may be more or less impossible, even undesirable, to be particularly confident about oneself. The journey a human has to go through between the ages of ten and twenty is necessarily traumatic in its degrees of oddity, intensity and embarrassment. During this span, a person might double in weight, grow seven centimetres in some years, discover sex, be covered in acne, learn to live on their own, experiment with hating their parents, properly realise that they are going to die and take on board that life is infinitely bleaker, and yet also more exciting and rich, than they had ever guessed.

No wonder that teenagers often speak in an extremely low voice and need to spend a lot of time in the shadows. They are – or should be – digesting a host of hugely daunting ideas. They might be appalled by what is happening to their bodies and longing for the simplicities and comforts of childhood. They may be shocked by what the adult world has in store for them, while resenting everything they were not told about when they were smaller. They want Mummy and Daddy's love and at the same time long for these grotesque oldies to leave them alone and die. There might be some adolescents who can stride forth into reality with confidence, but we might almost worry about what they had missed if they did so.

The self-doubt and mood swings of those years are the secret guarantors of adult complexity. Those who have spent a lot of time in their rooms, written reams of excruciating poetry, made some bad mistakes, felt rejected by everyone and been sure that they didn't want to go on are the future creatives and visionaries the world will need. It is almost an infringement of good sense to feel utterly well at fifteen. We shouldn't worry about underconfident adolescents; we should worry more about those who lack the imagination to find those cursed years very taxing indeed.

Sian Davey, *Martha*, 2017

It is normal to assume that those who own the planes and the fancy cars, the penthouses and the yachts must be the confident ones among us. What solid and self-congratulatory types must be at the wheel of those Italian saloons and in the leather armchairs of those Gulfstream G700s.

But ownership of luxuries can mask something more complicated and, from certain angles, more poignant. It would seldom occur to anyone to seek so urgently to impress the world unless they had not first been afflicted by a stubborn sense of being superfluous and invisible. We may be tempted to read Ferraris and Riva speedboats as signs of wealth, but they could with greater accuracy be interpreted as symbols of a background impression of invisibility and sorrow. They are evidence of deprivation. How poor one would need to feel in order to make all the sacrifices required to accumulate a fortune; how humiliated one must at some point have been in order to demand preternatural respect and obedience from everyone in one's path.

It is an achievement of sorts for parents to give their children the means by which they can go on to build up a fortune. It is an even greater achievement to imbue them with such an innate sense of significance and worth that they are liberated from having to spend the greater part of their adult lives in search of status. True privilege involves transcending the craving for wealth; true luxury means being unbothered by simplicity.

There are, of course, ways of going without that are entwined with resentment and shame, but these should not obscure instances of genuine disinterest in the accoutrements of power; examples of people who are sufficiently at ease with themselves to ride a bike, paddle a canoe or live in a cottage. If envy were more correctly ascribed, these would be the proper targets of our aspiration and respect. These are the genuinely confident ones among us.

Slim Aarons, *Waterskiing from the Hotel Du Cap-Eden-Roc in Cap d'Antibes, France*, 1969

It isn't easy to stay confident in the modern city. Every day tends to bring with it fears that rivals may show up who are cannier, more energetic and more ruthless than we are. Someone else may unseat us with a better proposition or pitch. Paranoia and dread hang heavy in the midday heat. We're only ever a few wrong moves away from failure.

We're apt to interpret our worries very personally: we may be lacking guts or inspiration, focus or intelligence. Something is wrong with us. But in truth, far more than we generally allow ourselves to imagine, our worries are a consequence of the economic system we live within. We aren't reckless or weak; we are living under capitalism.

The way an economy is arranged not only determines what people do to earn money, it also regulates how they think and feel. Agricultural societies breed patience, conservatism and a respect for nature. Military societies throw the spotlight on honour and self-sacrifice. And our own world constantly bathes us in an atmosphere of competitiveness, envy and anxiety. In order to function optimally, market capitalism has to leave us feeling that we have not kept up, that someone, somewhere is about to destroy us, that we cannot rest for an instant and that every advantage is temporary and unstable. These aren't defects of the system; they are the system.

Furthermore, these vigilant attitudes can't neatly be left behind at the end of the working day; they infect everything from how we conduct relationships to how we parent our children, approach media or look at our bodies.

One way to regain confidence is to remind ourselves not to take our constant failures of confidence so personally. We are flawed, no doubt, but more than this, we are living inside a system with a genius for generating industrial quantities of fear. We aren't worried all the time because we are personally deficient; we're breathing poisoned air. The illness is general – and healing begins the moment we can be generous enough with ourselves to start to recognise it as such.

Lee Friedlander, *New York City*, 1990

Early in his career, the Swiss naturalist Conrad Gessner formulated an enviably ambitious plan: he would spend the rest of his life tracking down and describing every animal on the planet, from the armadillo to the green chameleon, the Egyptian mongoose to the rhinoceros. His labours resulted in one of the first and most beautiful works of zoology, *Historia animalium*, published in Zurich between 1551 and 1558.

Gessner got a lot of things wrong. He was muddled about names and numbers of legs. Many of his colours were off. He was confused about the number of stripes on the tiger and spots on the leopard. But it is Gessner's boldness that continues to impress. He didn't worry about the odd mistake, and nor did he limit his aspirations for fear of treading on other experts' toes.

He did have one enormous advantage, however: he was early on in the game. He did not have to suffer from the dispiriting sense – which too often consumes us today – that everything must surely already be known; that there is nothing at all we might think that hasn't already been better expressed somewhere else by someone else. The existence of so many books – 130 million – doesn't so much inspire us as crush us: what more could we possibly add? What thought worth having could ever germinate in our naive minds? The virgin snow across which Gessner once drove his intellectual sledge is now criss-crossed with others' tracks. Increased knowledge has decimated our intellectual self-confidence.

But this cannot, in truth, be fair, for we still don't understand so much: how to have good marriages, run countries, educate children, create beautiful architecture or overcome loneliness – just to start the list. We have mapped less than one-billionth of the real map of knowledge. We are almost as much at the beginning as Gessner was. Nothing should legitimately stop us from imagining that we couldn't right now head out and, with a fair wind and a few years of toil, discover a menagerie of things at once unknown, colourful and essential.

Conrad Gessner, *Hedgehog*, hand-coloured woodcut, from *Historia animalium*, 1551

rinum uulǵq̄ nõ alter quàm ech
num interpretatur, Plinii fore
iniatus, a cuius qui terrestris est
erinaceum conuerti, Masi irius.
Ego aquatilem echinum à Lati
nis erinaceũ dici haũ uulgo lo-
dicitũ nũ terrestrem ũnma
rinum appellãt pro erico per a
pharesin, Quamobrem & Mas
sarium mirori, sic cum impro-
pri uocat cum branchia nõ ha
beat, melius quidam offerisad
numerant, erinaceũ Latine ui
cari scribit. Herinaceus qui &
herix, & hericius, quod spini
horreant dici, ut quidam uolͤr,
Perottus. Herice, quod spinis
horreat,Grapaldus. Herich, qua
& echini dicuntur. Eucherius,
Varoni inuenisse scericium cum
proboscide scribit, ut Nonius d́
tat ex Varronis Sexagͤ, his uo
bis, Inuenissé scericium procul
cũ dormiret cõ
caluum esse factum ericium pi
pisse, tam glaber quàmborices
lis, aliis cum proboscide. Syllat
ticus barbare iriccium protulit
Implicituḿ sibu spinoli corp
Nemeliauus,
kpod Hebraice herinaceũ fo
nat: quam uocem licet alii alite
interpretentur,herinacei tame
esse constat: quoniam medici ut
Serapion, Sylua ticus, & alii qu
Arabice scripserunt, quod qu
pellant (apud Auiceñam caste
scribitur) & Graecorum de che
no terrestri uerba eius mentio
adscribunt. R. Dauid Kimhi a
uem solitudine gaudentem in
terpretatur, quam Ioseph Kim
pater Dauidis Arabice uocat
uulgo cartag
(id est testudo, sed inepte ut u
deur cum pro aue ponatur fo
ce turtur legendum, quæ uulg
ubiq́ fere nomen Latinum reti
net,& solitaria auis est,) Id&Ki
hi Sophonie, lingua Ismaëlitic

(inqui) dicitur, Arabice, addit Esaiæ 14, semper in aquis uersari, Salomon
eat, alludens puto ad Gallicam uocem herisson, id est hericium, secuus nimirũ nostros interpre
Nam Septuaginta Esaiæ 14, & Sophonie uterum, Hieronymus hericium, Ita etiam Esaiæ
ubi Salomon aurum dicit zucera uel cuera, id est noctuam. Redigam Babylonem in posse
fionem erinacei, & in stagna aquarum, Esaiæ 14. Hebraicè kipod eltquod animal esse aquatile ũ el
tem quod iuxta aquas habiter, ex his concludi posse aliqui putant: & quoniam uerbũ præcederu
facidere Hebraist significat, eruditus quidam apud nos lurum,seu potius castorͤ, qui arbores sur
cidit, esse colligit. Ab hac uoce ultima tantum litera differ kipoz, quam R. Kimhi euider
cum kipod significationis exstimat, quonã zain & daleth crebro inter se permutantur,similiter Sa
lomon, Septuaginta, autem esse echinum, & Hieronymus hericium exponit. Abraham Esaia non lineͤr r
tione resiliũ, autem esse concedens. Nam Esaiæ 34, autem esse apparet ex eo quod aliis rebus autũ
nomin

The problem with libraries is that they can be so large, impressive and filled with knowledge that they unwittingly embed in us an idea that everything worth registering, everything valuable and true, must lie 'out there', must already have been classed on a shelf with an index number to await our discovery the moment we cease to be so preoccupied with ourselves.

But what this modest, respectful and quietly self-hating conclusion disguises is that each one of us is an unparalleled and superlative centre of knowledge in and of ourselves; our minds have more ideas stored in them than are to be found in the collective catalogues of the Biblioteca Geral da Universidade de Coimbra, the Morgan Library in New York and the British Library in London; we have vaults filled with a greater number of moving and beautiful scenes than those of the world's grandest museums put together. We are just failing to wander the stacks and galleries as often as we should; we are failing to notice what we have seen. So convinced are we that insights of worth lie beyond us, that we have omitted to consult the treasury of thoughts and visions generated every hour by our endlessly brilliant, fatefully unexplored minds.

The American essayist Ralph Waldo Emerson once remarked: 'In the minds of geniuses, we find – once more – our own neglected thoughts.' In other words, geniuses don't have thoughts that are in the end so very different from our own; they have simply had the confidence to take them more seriously. Rather than imagining that their minds are only a pale shadow of the minds of infinitely greater thinkers who lived and died elsewhere long ago, they have been respectful enough of their existence to conceive that one or two properly valuable ideas might plausibly choose to alight in the familiar aviary of their own intelligences. Thinking is – in a way we generally refuse to imagine – a truly democratic activity.

We all have very similar and very able minds; where geniuses differ is in their more confident inclinations to study them properly.

Candida Höfer, *Biblioteca Geral da Universidade de Coimbra IV*, 2006

What many of us would dearly love to do, if only we had the confidence, is to start our own business. But here, as in so many other fields, what may deter us is a dispiriting feeling that everything has surely already been done; the world obviously doesn't need yet another bakery, supermarket, pet shop or skin cream manufacturer.

But such pessimism is a sign of a punishingly and misguidedly narrow conception of what business is actually for. The ultimate purpose of business is to satisfy human needs. Put more colloquially, it is to make people happy. And once we frame matters like this, what we quickly see is that business as a whole hasn't begun to fulfil its historic mission – because human beings are still so pervasively, fascinatingly and (if one can put it this way) inspiringly miserable.

There are, of course, a few areas where enterprises have learnt to satisfy our needs rather well. The world truly doesn't require yet another brand of breakfast cereal. The toilet roll market is saturated. We have enough white T-shirts, trainers or baked beans.

But if we're looking to identify entrepreneurial gaps, we need only run through an average day and note all the areas in which we remain unfulfilled. Despite the millions of businesses that exist, there is still no one to call when our partner falls into a sulk. Almost no one seems to offer us a service to alleviate the Sunday blues. There aren't any enterprises helping us to have interesting conversations. There aren't any multinationals promising us next-day delivery on better parent–child relations. In short, across a vast range of areas, we're still scrambling to align the disciplines of commerce and industry with the intimate pains and hopes of our minds and bodies.

Every area of frustration, grief, friction, longing and boredom is a business waiting to be born. Profit is merely the reward for superior insight into the unformed wishes of strangers. Entrepreneurialism has barely got off the ground, let alone run its course.

Homer Sykes, *Family corner shop, Brick Lane, London*, 1974

At the beginning of the 14th century, the leaders of an obscure Tuscan town on the banks of the Arno River formulated a plan as visionary as it turned out to be historically significant: they set their sights on turning Florence into one of the great centres of commerce, art, architecture and scholarship. They wished – extraordinarily given its standing at the time – that their town would become the equal of Venice and Rome, Paris or – most impudently of all – ancient Athens.

More surprisingly still, they succeeded beyond every conceivable measure. In the next 200 years, Florence's language was adopted as the vernacular in the whole of the Italian peninsula; its leading architect, Filippo Brunelleschi, invented modern engineering; its artistic culture gave birth to Michelangelo, Leonardo da Vinci, Botticelli and Giotto; its local currency, the florin, became the global reserve currency; its scholars rediscovered classical literature and its navigator, Amerigo Vespucci, lent his name to two continents.

One cannot ascribe Florence's success to any of the standard features associated with urban renewal: the town was not – at the outset – especially rich; it had no particular natural resources; it was militarily weak and surrounded by rivals. What Florence's success can ultimately be attributed to was an ingredient that sounds hugely peculiar, improbable and plain naive when stated baldly: *confidence*. One of the great cities of the world arose off the back of an inspired mood. It wasn't coal, guns or wealth that did it: it was a movement of the mind.

The idea is both momentous and terrifying, for it forces us to acknowledge that all that separates us from a golden age might be the right degree of self-belief. We cannot keep making excuses. Right now, if we could only align the molecules of our brains appropriately, our generation could create structures to rival Brunelleschi's and artworks to stand besides those of Michelangelo. We could stop being tourists of past greatness and become great ourselves.

We remain mediocre not for any immovable reasons; we are simply overlooking what we could do if we rediscovered a way to dream.

Florence, Italy, 2020

One of the unlikeliest ideas we can entertain of people, especially those we are drawn to or respect, is that they might, beneath it all, be lonely. We know so much about our own sense of isolation: how it has been with us from the start, began in Reception, haunted us all through school, didn't quite leave us at university and has dogged us intermittently throughout our adult lives. We know how badly we ache to find an echo in others' hearts of a range of our own fears and melancholy insights.

However, we are terrified that, were we to try to unburden ourselves, we would be met with puzzlement or jollity or changes of subject. The loneliness of others remains an abstract, almost unreal proposition. It simply doesn't seem plausible that many of the feelings of freakishness and shame we know so well might be besetting friends, acquaintances or thoughtful-looking strangers we pass by in the street. We are all such masters at conveying purpose, invulnerability, good cheer and busyness. We have congenital difficulties letting on about the grave difficulties of being human.

What should make us feel more confident – and therefore readier to reach out to others – is that there are so many very good reasons why anyone decent might be lonely: because social life is governed by appalling pressures to lie and disguise one's real state of mind; because the conditions of existence – fairly considered – should breed despair and misanthropy; because our ideas are far stranger but also sweeter, kinder and sillier than we know how to admit.

We hold back from other people because we refuse the thought that they might be as troubled and sad as we are. What should stop us being so reserved – and at moments give us the courage to build friendships and begin love affairs – is not a sudden burst of steeliness, but a stronger conviction that everyone else is necessarily, deep down, as messed up and craving reassurance as we are. We might more often dare to say hello.

Garry Winogrand, *New York*, 1967

It's a truth universally acknowledged that a normal person in search of a holiday will enjoy skiing; they will delight in the bracing mountain air, thrill at going down mogul-dotted slopes and feel pleasantly exhausted after a day of parallel turns. This assumption about pleasure joins a host of others proposed by the modern world. Normal people will equally enjoy white wine, the Amalfi Coast, the novels of Margaret Atwood, dogs, high heels, small children, Miami Beach, oral sex, Banksy, marriage, Netflix and vegetarianism.

We may legitimately delight in all of these elements; the issue lies in the immense pressure we are under to do so. The truth about ourselves may, in reality, be a great deal more mysterious than the official narrative allows. Whatever our commitments to decorum and good order, we may be, in our depths, far more distinctive than we're supposed to be. We may – once we become sensitive to our faint tremors of authentic delight and boredom – hate the idea of jogging, the theatre, business school, jazz, tattoos, flossing or meeting other people's dogs. We might find Paris and New York unbearable, while conversely get a kick out of staying home and reading the novels of Stendhal, baking apricot cakes and chatting to the over-80s. Our pleasures may be situated in some profoundly unheralded and unfashionable corners.

We tend to be so shy about who we actually are. We repress our nascent wish to go plane spotting. We don't admit to many people that we'd like to be in bed by 9 p.m. Or are interested in visiting nuclear power stations. Or might want to take a holiday in Turkmenistan or Gabon.

We are, each one of us, fetishists of varied kinds, but fetishists without the confidence to acknowledge the singular nature of our delights. If we realise we are at odds with our peers, if we secretly start to despise what they adore, if we turn down Kitzbuhel, we aren't merely being capricious; we're growing into ourselves. Acquiring a reputation as a weirdo is no cause for alarm; it's a sign that we are – at last – developing a character.

Dede Johnston, *Ski Day, Kitzbuhel*, 2017

Shortly before completing a study of some delightful pigeons that had come to keep him company on the balcony of his villa in Vallauris in the South of France, Picasso observed a group of young children in a classroom painting with particular exuberance and vitality. 'At their age,' he rued, 'I knew how to paint like Titian. It's taken me a lifetime to relearn to paint like them.'

That Picasso, one of the most courageous of all artistic figures, should have confessed to an occasional struggle to create with simplicity and emotional candour tells us a lot about how in thrall we can all be to unnecessary ideas of respectability and elaboration – across every area of our lives. We tend to overcomplicate matters out of a timid fear that our true feelings, gestures and thoughts might not be enough on their own. In art, we lean on academic ideas of propriety; in literature, we use dense, obfuscatory language; in cookery, we prepare heavy, convoluted meals; in conversation, we talk in abstract terms that cover up the intensity and vulnerability of our actual feelings.

It takes a great deal of confidence to strip out what is superfluous, showy and emotionally cloaked. We find it hard to imagine that who we are could really be enough.

We're scared about plainly revealing just what we find beautiful or sweet. We can't imagine that the simple meals of bread, olives and cheese that we love might also appeal to others. We hesitate for an age to tell those we care about what they truly mean to us.

We tend to get a little better at directness as we grow older; it's no surprise that a great many artists have become more 'primitive' (and in the process a good deal more engaging) with time; as death comes closer, they have found the strength and seriousness to leave 'good' manners behind. We should aim for a comparable evolution, learning to live guilelessly and directly, saying more of what we feel, crying when we should and expressing ourselves with the profundity and jubilance of the small children we once were.

Pablo Picasso, *The Pigeons*, c. 1957

63

When it comes to deciding what to do with our lives, we are frequently presented with what looks like a very painful choice: the passionate path vs the safe path. The latter involves the slow mastery of a dependable profession; we will be bored, but we know we'll never be fired. Meanwhile, the former is a high-wire act in which we fantasise about generating an income from what we deeply love and yet we constantly fear penury and humiliation.

The choice can feel acute, but it may be less so than it seems, once we properly explore the concept of safety. We are never properly safe so long as we are doing something we hate or are pursuing out of cowardice. In the deeply competitive conditions of modernity, our back-up career – the one we adopt out of fear – will be someone else's central ambition; our plan B will be someone else's plan A, which places us at an immediate disadvantage in terms of the energy and focus we are able to muster. The 'safe' choice might ruin us.

By contrast, what we love is what we are obsessed by anyway; we'd do it for free – which decisively increases our chances of mastery while reducing the price of failure. A decade of mixed results on a passion project is inherently less onerous than unspectacular returns for a whole career in a hateful field.

It is in the end not very safe to use the one life we have forcing ourselves to do what we know from the outset we won't enjoy – simply in order to keep living. This isn't safety; it's masochism. We may all have to spend our first two decades suffering through the education system, but at some point, we are allowed to leave school; at some point, we need to have a shot at answering what life could be about beyond obedience and timidity.

It is not very common to have a passion; most of us don't. Yet if we are blessed enough to have one, we are risking far more than we should by failing to heed its call.

London Bridge, Rush hour, 1930

What if we don't have a calling? When deciding on our futures, we have tendencies to panic and quickly lose confidence in ourselves if we can't say what we would like to do with our professional lives. We assume that being confused about our career goals is a sign that we cannot have any intrinsic interests and so must settle immediately on a dull but steady path.

To help us hold our nerve, we should think of our careers via the metaphor of archaeology. Archaeologists do not generally expect to dig fully intact vessels out of the ground; they presume them to be smashed and scattered and understand that their principle task is one of sifting and reassembly. They will take a confused medley of unprepossessing shards and try to fit them into a coherent whole with patience and imagination. Their job is to wonder what conceivable pot the fragment they are holding might belong to.

Few of us know from the outset exactly what we want to be; few of us can dig out a whole named career from the soil of our unconscious. Instead, we just encounter shards of interest that are symptoms of wider goals that are not yet arranged into anything we can point to as a destiny. All we meet with day to day are tiny moments of heightened delight, curiosity or excitement. We need to learn to look after these with meticulous care and constantly ask ourselves to what totality they might belong. The assemblage is unlikely to be obvious: a deep compassion for sick animals might, in time, emerge as a symptom of an underlying vocation for psychotherapy, a joy at managing a school club might gradually take its place as evidence of an aptitude for running the finances of a company.

Our real selves are jumbled; our destinies are buried like the fragments of a shattered pot. But we should have the confidence to believe that they will one day present a fulfilling whole – and so give ourselves the time and encouragement to gather their disparate parts.

Attic black-figure volute-krater, known as
the François Vase, c. 570–565 BCE

If we wanted to imagine what confidence looked like, we could do worse than to opt for a small masterpiece by Pierre Bonnard painted in northern France in the summer of 1909.

It takes a moment to find her, but when we do, we know at once who the heroine is and what the true point of Bonnard's work might be. What charms us about the little girl with flowers in her hair and a ripe green apple in her hand is how blithe, indifferent and cheerful she has managed to remain, despite everything. The sky is not entirely clear, but she is in the sunlight and her mood is upbeat and purposeful. The wheat fields have ripened, the flowers are blooming, the fruit trees are laden. The world may be vast and complicated and filled with much that is disagreeable and tragic, but this is no time for despair or melancholy: the girl's eyes are solely on her apple and the path ahead. She doesn't care about the big city in the distance, with its competitiveness, snobbery and self-importance. Let that ugly conurbation remain an unknown smudge for as long as it can. Nor does she care a jot about the train down in the valley, hurrying madly to its destination, occasionally bellowing a frantic call as it speeds to deliver its coal or iron ore to the docks of Le Havre or Dunkirk.

When we are being kind to ourselves, we are all a version of this jocund girl. We know about pain, dread and confusion, and appreciate that they may return to haunt us soon enough. But, for a time, we can keep them at bay to focus on our own path and purpose – and on green apples. We don't have to care who is looking or what others are doing. We don't need always to take everyone else's burdens on board.

Bonnard's unassuming genius guides us back to the landscape we belong to whenever fear abates.

Pierre Bonnard, *Train and Barges*, 1909

For a long time, we just smiled and said 'yes' to pretty much everything and everyone: parents, school, peers, colleagues, strangers. We smiled because no one had ever granted us a right not to. Then gradually, after years of pain and, perhaps, an eventual crisis, we started to imagine that we might after all dare to push back. We learnt that there might be a way to be at once kind and firm. There could be a way to tell an adolescent child that the continuous rudeness was now enough. Or an elderly parent that their messages were manipulative. Or a partner that we couldn't take their clever lies any longer. Or a colleague at work that our role wasn't solely to make it easy for them to be lazy. Or a stranger at the laundrette that we don't feel like engaging in small talk about the weather or their holiday to Barcelona.

Self-assertion terrifies us, of course: *If I speak up, they will hate me; if I speak up, I will become a target for retribution; if I speak up, I will feel intolerably mean.* Many of us didn't have the sort of childhood that allowed us to protest with an easy conscience. Our role was to stand back and let other people play out their antics: they were the ones who could shout and threaten – we just had to be very still and do our homework.

But in reality, people don't tend to hate those who have boundaries; they respect and like them more. They feel in the presence of a maturity and authoritativeness that appear worthy of their time; they trust those who call out their deceit.

We may have already spent a large chunk of our lives in a passive relationship to the world, but we aren't a piece of helpless flotsam on the river of others' wishes; we have agency, direction and a rudder. We might take on board a highly implausible yet redemptive notion: that we can be accepted and, at the same time, when the occasion demands it, as it probably will a few times every day, have the right to utter a warm-sounding, gentle and definitive 'no'.

Julie Mathers, *With In #II*, date unknown

Every morning, for close to a decade, we stood waiting for the bus to school. It was the same routine summer and winter; the shell-shocked awakening, the feeling of resignation, the raucous meanness of our peers on the twenty-minute drive over. It shaped our whole mentality.

So much so that we may be finding it uncommonly hard, now that we are in our third, fourth or even fifth decade, to come to a realisation that sounds entirely obvious while being, in reality, truly incomprehensible to our deeper selves: we have actually left school.

We may know well enough that we have left the physical premises behind, but that doesn't stop us from remaining trapped within the mentality that schools breed and sustain. To start with, we may be suffering from a pernicious degree of respect for authority. We keep imagining – in the same way we did when we were nine – that 'other people' know. Somewhere out there, there are answers and, even if we don't grasp what they are, it isn't our role, as it wasn't in Mrs Sharp's classroom, to start to question the whole foundations of anything. Furthermore, if it's presently horrible, if we're bored and frustrated, if we're plodding through our tasks without spirit, that's no cause for alarm; that's the way it should be – and always was. The point isn't to have fun; it's to do what you're told.

We're doing this for someone else anyway: *You have to shine. We've given you so much.* What matters is the performance, not any inner sense of satisfaction. 'They' want what is good for us and speak on behalf of our long-term interests. *Look at how your peers are performing. Don't think you could ever know better; distrust your instincts. We'll look after you. Follow the rules; you will thrive.*

It's time to stop. It's time to properly graduate. Our weariness is telling us that something is very wrong. We need to stop waiting for the school bus – and begin our free adult lives.

Greg Miller, *Kalyani*, 2016

It's one of the telling quirks of history that, just as the world was growing ever noisier and more urbanised, there arose – in many countries of Europe – an obsession with hermits: bearded men in long, unkempt cloaks who lived on their own, normally in a forest or up a mountainside, reading, reflecting and contemplating nature. It briefly became a fashion among 18th-century aristocrats to build – and staff – hermitages on their estates. Charles Hamilton, the English owner of Painshill Park in Surrey, offered the then enormous sum of £700 to anyone who would agree to spend seven years as a hermit in a hut on his grounds, on the condition that he spoke to no one and never cut his hair (though after only three weeks, the successful candidate was discovered chatting in a local pub and sacked).

Hermits fascinate us because they are who we might be if only we learnt to be braver. They have unearthed the courage to be unusual. They have ceased relying on outside sources of esteem in order to value themselves. They are free.

But it pays to remember that hermits were almost certainly something else before they reached a state of liberation: they were probably followers of fashion, panickers about trends and people who minded rather a lot what was being uttered about them on the street. It's unusual to be born not caring what others think. Such indifference is only ever the result of immense psychological labour; the 18th century had the wisdom to recognise it as an achievement to be ranked alongside – or indeed far above – winning a battle or making a fortune.

Being a hermit ultimately has nothing to do with letting one's hair grow or maintaining years of silence. These are blunt, external symbols of what really counts: a state of mind in which we make conscious efforts to distance ourselves from the absurdities of our era and focus on what remains beautiful, kind and good in the time that remains.

Hermits had a reputation for being strange; on closer examination, we should wonder why anyone would ever fail to want to be one.

Gerrit Dou, *A Hermit*, 1661

Some of what can render us excessively timid professionally is the fear of what might happen to us if things went wrong. We vaguely but powerfully picture the most lurid scenarios resulting from a sacking or bankruptcy: being forced to move to a monstrous housing project on the edge of town, wearing rags, needing to beg ...

But confidence might return if we could only hold back our panicked thoughts for long enough to explore with greater imagination what could in reality still be possible without much of what we now consider indispensable. We stand to discover that, though a fall in station might not be desirable, it never needs to justify panic.

Many of us could live on a salary drastically lower than our current one and still benefit from sufficient beauty and dignity. A long-standing tradition in Japanese architecture proposes that a simple hut can – when properly thought through – be charming and elegant. When he took stock of his limited resources, Takeshi Hosaka did not despair; using a combination of steel sheeting, concrete and wood, he created aesthetic delight on a plot no larger than a parking space. One can imagine similarly inspiring exercises in thoughtful renunciations around food, clothes or holidays.

Our societies surround us with rags-to-riches stories – ostensibly to lend us confidence. But we would benefit far more from well-chosen riches-to-rags stories that show us successful transitions from prosperity to noble simplicity.

The whole thrust of industrialisation has been to democratise access to consumer goods and make it possible to live adequately on little. But the benefits of our herculean material labours have simultaneously been destroyed by unnecessary psychological suggestions that only an upper-middle-class life will do.

We have been scared into conservatism because we are not thinking straight about the consequences of so-called failure. Risks will no longer seem impossible once we properly accept that, contrary to what we are continually told, a graceful life might not be dependent on a fortune.

Takeshi Hosaka, Microhome, Tokyo, 2019

It is possible to catch a telling glimpse of our levels of underconfidence in a sad quirk of our approach to social life: our inability to leave a party. By which one really means, to leave a party when we desperately want to, when we are exhausted and have a daunting day ahead of us.

Why don't we just leave? Chiefly, because we very badly need people to like us, and we cannot possibly imagine that they would unless we did precisely – down to the last degree – what they ask of us. We wouldn't dare not to laugh at their jokes; we would never risk contradicting their political views – and we certainly wouldn't hazard asking them where the toilet was or departing early from one of their celebrations. People need a lot of self-love before they can find their own needs acceptable and, by extension, dare to try to transmit these to others.

We, the reluctant party-leavers, strongly suspect that there is, deep down, something very bad about us – akin to a foul odour – that needs to be repeatedly apologised for and cannot possibly be compounded by starting to say what we want. We know just how much they would talk about us the minute the door closed, because we appreciate how much there is to say: how repulsive we look, how nervous we are, how sexually weird we seem, what losers we are turning into.

In short, we don't leave the party because we hate ourselves a lot – and we do so principally because we weren't sufficiently loved by those close to us in the key early years as our self-image was taking shape.

The good news is that if we do ever dare to get our coat and go, we'll know at once that we did the right thing. The dark, cold street will welcome us. The majestic trees will greet us. The stars will embolden us. No one cares.

The party is not – of course – just the party; it's the job we hate, the relationship that's making us ill and the parent who bullies us. We don't, in reality, ever have to stay. We need, above anything else, to be more loyal to ourselves.

Tod Papageorge, from *Studio 54*, 1978–1980

Our dips in confidence can have an unlikely-sounding source: hope. We become hopeful that things can turn out well and that we will get through events without setback and frustration, but then, when life turns out to be trickier than we'd budgeted for, we fall prey to grave panic, despair and anger.

We end up defeated because we expect – in the background – that people will be kind, that those we try to date will be reliable, that parents will be mature, that colleagues will be grateful and dedicated, that it will be easy to write a book, that finding a profession will be simple, that the political process will be intelligent, that the media will be subtle, that the trains will run on time, that our children will be kind and that the holidays will bring rest and respite.

We are being reckless. In order to dampen our cycles of hope and sadness, and all the wounds to our self-esteem and sense of balance these entail, we need to turn ourselves into misanthropes. The last thing young people aspiring to a life of action and resilience should be hearing about is happiness. We become strong through well-targeted doses of gloom. In this regard, the United States, the most monomaniacally optimistic country on earth, does its citizens an enormous disservice – promising them that nothing less than contentment might be within reach, and thereby condemning them to ongoing, unnecessary doses of alienation and rage.

To build up confidence, the young need from an early age to be taught that love is largely a chimera, that workplace success will be elusive, that anxiety is more or less permanent, that the species is wicked and the political process decadent; only against such a pitch-black backdrop will the inevitable frustrations they will encounter seem, not as now, violations of a contract, but ordinary and, for the most part, masterable hurdles they were waiting for from the start.

The 18th-century French essayist Chamfort observed that a man should swallow a toad every morning to be sure of not meeting with anything more revolting in the day ahead. To properly guard one's sanguinity, a handful of toads might be advised.

Brian Shumway, *Happy Valley*, 2014

It can be hard not to panic in a plane on its way down to the ground in a thunderstorm. It isn't easy to watch out of the window as the aircraft descends through 3 kilometres of agitated stratus and cumulonimbus clouds streaked with occasional forks of lightning – and as agonised sounds emerge from somewhere deep within the fuselage, as though a saw was dementedly cutting the craft in two. It seems like an approach to Hades through the fires of Hephaestus. Then, when it seems it couldn't possibly get any worse, the plane rises as if it has been seized by a wilful giant and then is slammed vindictively down onto the runway; fourteen tyres hitting the ground at 270 kilometres per hour, releasing a monstrous roar that promises immediate annihilation in an inferno of fuel and divine anger.

Except, of course, that flight 765 inbound from Toronto was never in the slightest danger. This is standard procedure for landing at dusk in a minor equinoctial storm. The two pilots remember what they went through on the approach to Antigua last September; now that was interesting!

Machines survive not through luck or supernatural favour, but because they have been meticulously endowed with what engineers call 'tolerance', a capacity to withstand stresses many times larger than those they ordinarily encounter: planes have wings that can flex 5 metres; they can land in crosswinds of 96 kilometres per hour; they can fly across a continent on only one engine. They are designed for crises.

And so, rather surprisingly, are we. We survived immense evolutionary pressures to make it this far. We're not so easy to finish off. There are moments of profound despair and of certainty of collapse. But then there is the next day.

Most things that look like the end are not the end. We're thrown around, we swear we are going to succumb, we anticipate our demise in the darkness. But we endure. Our inner navigator gets us down. We make it home.

KLM Boeing 777 landing in bad weather, 2020

It's a measure of how woefully and comedically melodramatic we are that we need this picture very badly indeed. It should, with justice, be placed in every school, bedroom, airport and government office in the world.

It was taken at 4.48 a.m. (GMT) on 14th February 1990 when the Voyager 1 space probe – travelling at 64,000 kilometres per hour, having left Earth back in September 1977 – reached the edge of our solar system, 6,054,587,000 kilometres away from home. The craft turned around and pointed its 1,500-millimetre high-resolution narrow-angle camera back at our planet – and saw it, famously, as a grain of sand, less than one pixel in size, in the murky infinity of the cosmos.

Voyager 1 had all kinds of scientific experiments to carry out for NASA; one of its primary responsibilities was to examine Saturn and its moons. But thanks to this image, a less heralded, more incidental and yet no less significant role opened up for it: to help human beings to remain calm when they have a lunch appointment with an important business colleague, or when they are inviting someone on a date, or having sex for the first time, or giving a speech to a tough audience, or making a difficult call to a client.

NASA's miraculous machine was on hand to offer a corrective to our ruinous feelings of self-importance and significance, upon which so much of our unnecessary panic and timidity rests. With quiet eloquence, NASA's dot was reminding us that we are – mercifully – a very small deal indeed in the totality of time and space.

We are just a piece of mysterious, purposeless biological matter clinging to a minuscule spinning rock somewhere in one spiral-shaped corner of a galaxy filled with 100 billion planets in a universe destined to come to a close in the blink of an eye in 22 billion years' time. From beyond Neptune, no one can see how embarrassed we are; no one minds how sad we have been. It doesn't matter how unloved we were in childhood or how many errors we have made.

We aren't inherently anxious or resolutely underconfident; we have just been standing far too close for far too long.

Voyager 1 space probe, *Pale Blue Dot*; *Earth from 6 billion kilometres*, 1990 (Earth is the speck halfway up the right-hand band)

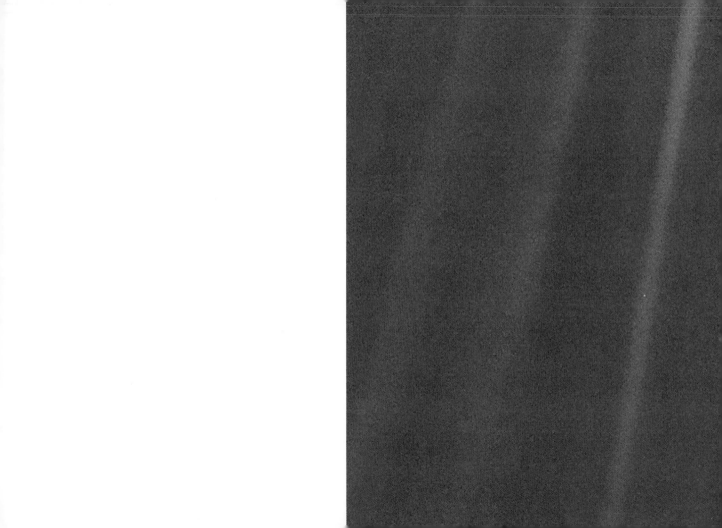

We often hold ourselves back from our more courageous ventures with a frightened and stern question: *What if I am – in fact – an idiot?* To which kindly voices will tend to reply that naturally we are far from being any such thing: we're clever, we work hard, we're beautiful inside.

However, if confidence is the goal, a starkly different yet far more effective route to reassurance is to be recommended. We shouldn't focus on whether or not we're idiots. We can take it for granted that, of course, we are. But the good news is: so is everyone else. We're on a planet of 8 billion idiots. Everyone we see is substantially unreasonable and foolish. There go the parents, messing up another generation by failing to understand their own minds; there are the businesspeople, creating money out of unnecessary desires; there are the schoolteachers, instructing people for a life they haven't fathomed themselves; there are the scientists, helping people to live longer who haven't even grasped how to be good right now; there are the lovers, as passionate about, as they are unaware of, what love means.

To think we have any reason to be scared of our idiocy in such company! If we tried to ask someone to have dinner with us and we were rejected, or tried to write a book and no one liked it, or started a business and turnover was slow, we'd only be joining a line of idiots that would snake to Jupiter and back.

We don't need to suffer from impostor syndrome; there is no one properly sensible that anyone could in truth grow into. We are all just a collection of clueless, overexcited primates. No one is normal; no one is sane.

To bolster our strength, we should begin every day by repeating: *I have been an idiot before, I am an idiot now and I will be an idiot again.* Thereafter, we will know to be a lot less frightened of losing our dignity. We – and the other 8 billion – never deserved any of it in the first place.

Pieter Bruegel the Elder, *The Blind Leading the Blind*, 1568

We grow underconfident and scared because we systematically miss the one thing we should ever really be frightened about. This isn't whether or not our date is going to call back, or if a colleague will mind if we present them with a proposal, or if we can leave a long-term relationship that no longer delivers intimacy or kindness. These things may well be slightly daunting, but the idea that they should terrify us, hold us back and stifle us for decades betokens a fundamental misunderstanding of the nature of existence.

There is, in reality, only one thing to fear – and we should fear it very much indeed, pretty much every day and, if possible, every hour. We should fear death because it comes around a great deal faster than we think; it seldom gives us much warning; it shows no consideration for what we might be in the middle of doing; it's blithely unconcerned with wealth, reputation, kindness or youth; it rudely pushes aside every delicate idea and tender intention – and blocks its ears to all pleas for clemency. It comes when it comes and does what it needs to, as it's been doing for millennia, hacking, chopping, decimating, pulverising. We're a skeleton already; we're just choosing to think about something else.

How demented, therefore, to keep worrying what the neighbours will think, to wonder whether what we're wearing will look OK, to agonise over whether we might have said something silly, to fret that we haven't got enough status. All this when, right behind us, somewhere in the shadows, is a hooded, psychopathic figure with a black cloak and a razor-sharp scythe.

The ultimate way to greater confidence isn't to do away with fear; it's to replace a litany of minuscule, life-sapping conventional fears with a single cataclysmic terror. We should petrify ourselves into courage.

There is, in the end, only one thing to be afraid of. Everything else deserves our confidence.

Robert Dighton, *Life and Death Contrasted*, 1784

89

Illustration List

p. 11 Rania Matar, *Georgina, Roxbury, Massachusetts*, 2010 © Rania Matar

p. 13   Lady Ottoline Morrell, Maria Huxley (née Nys), Lytton Strachey, Duncan Grant, Vanessa Bell © National Portrait Gallery, London

p. 15   Vincent van Gogh, *Café Terrace at Night*, 1888. Oil on canvas, 80.7 × 65.3 cm. Kröller-Müller Museum, Otterlo, The Netherlands. Giorgio Morara / Alamy Stock Photo

p. 17 Martin Parr, *Beach Therapy*, 2018 © Martin Parr / Magnum Photos

p. 19 Sophie Bassouls, *James Baldwin on the Quai des Grands Augustins, Paris*, April 1972 © Sophie Bassouls

p. 21 Pete Souza, *US President Obama and Ella Rhodes, daughter of Deputy National Security Advisor Ben Rhodes, White House*, October 2015. Official White House / Photo by Pete Souza. Courtesy Barack Obama Presidential Library

p. 23 Marcel Proust, manuscript pages, *In Search of Lost Time*, 1909

p. 25 Lumière Cinematograph, 1895 © National Science & Media Museum / Science & Society Picture Library. All rights reserved

p. 27 Tony Blair, St John's College, Oxford, 1972

p. 29 Bill Brandt, *Parlourmaid and Under-Parlourmaid Ready to Serve Dinner*, 1938. © Bill Brandt Archive

p. 31 Bronzino, *Portrait of a Young Man*, 1530s. Oil on wood, 96 × 75 cm. The Metropolitan Museum of Art, New York, USA

p. 33 Étienne Carjat, *Victor Hugo*, 1876. Bibliothèque nationale de France / Wikimedia Commons

p. 35 Mary Cassatt, *Mother and Child*, 1914. Pastel on wove paper mounted on canvas, 67.6 × 57.2 cm. The Metropolitan Museum of Art, New York, USA © 2023. Image © The Metropolitan Museum of Art / Art Resource / Scala, Florence

p. 37 Chancellor Angela Merkel of Germany with her husband, Joachim Sauer, 2013. 360b / Shutterstock.com

p. 39 Bonito tuna, reliquary fish, Santa Ana, Solomon Islands, early 20th century © Musée du quai Branly - Jacques Chirac, Dist. RMN-Grand Palais / Patrick Gries / Valérie Torre

p. 41 Diana Markosian, *Worshippers pray to the Virgin Mary in the village of Medjugorje, Bosnia and Herzegovina*, 2015 © Diana Markosian

p. 43 Andy Bishop, *Lively child and exasperated mother*, date unknown, Alamy Stock Photo

p. 45 Sian Davey, *Martha*, 2017 © Sian Davey

p. 47 Slim Aarons, *Waterskiing from the Hotel Du Cap-Eden-Roc in Cap d'Antibes, France*, 1969. Photo by Slim Aarons / Getty Images

p. 49 Lee Friedlander, *New York City*, 1990 © Lee Friedlander, courtesy Fraenkel Gallery, San Francisco and Luhring Augustine, New York

p. 51 Conrad Gessner, *Hedgehog*, hand-coloured woodcut, from *Historia animalium*, 1551

p. 53 Candida Höfer, *Biblioteca Geral da Universidade de Coimbra IV*, 2006. Photo © Christie's Images / Bridgeman Images / © Candida Höfer / VG Bild-Kunst, Bonn and DACS, London 2023

p. 55 Homer Sykes, *Family corner shop, Brick Lane, London*, 1974. Homer Sykes / Alamy Stock Photo

p. 57 Florence, Italy, 2020. Delpixel / Shutterstock.com

p. 59 Garry Winogrand, *New York*, 1967 © The Estate of Garry Winogrand, courtesy Fraenkel Gallery, San Francisco

p. 61 Dede Johnston, *Ski Day, Kitzbuhel*, 2017. Courtesy of Dede Johnston and TAG Fine Arts

p. 63 Pablo Picasso, *The Pigeons*, c. 1957. Colour lithograph, 99 × 66 cm. Photo © Christie's Images / Bridgeman Images / © Succession Picasso / DACS, London 2023

p. 65 London Bridge, Rush hour, 1930. The Print Collector / Alamy Stock Photo

p. 67 Attic black-figure volute-krater, known as the François Vase, c. 570-565 BCE. Bridgeman Images

p. 69 Pierre Bonnard, *Train and Barges*, 1909. Oil on canvas, 77 × 108 cm. Hermitage Museum, Saint Petersburg, Russia / Wikimedia Commons

p. 71 Julie Mathers, *With In #II*, date unknown
© Julie Mathers / Copyright Agency / DACS 2023

p. 73 Greg Miller, *Kalyani*, 2016 © Greg Miller

p. 75 Gerrit Dou, *A Hermit*, 1661. Oil on oak panel,
32.1 × 23.7 cm © Wallace Collection, London, UK /
Bridgeman Images

p. 77 Takeshi Hosaka, Microhome, Tokyo, 2019.
Koji Fujii / Takeshi Hosaka Architects / Nacasa
& Partners Inc

p. 79 Tod Papageorge, from *Studio 54*, New York,
1978–1980 © Tod Papageorge

p. 81 Brian Shumway, *Happy Valley*, 2014
© Brian Shumway

p. 83 KLM Boeing 777 landing in bad weather, 2020.
NurPhoto / Getty Images

p. 85 Voyager 1 space probe, *Pale Blue Dot; Earth
from 6 billion kilometres*, 1990. Voyager 1 / NASA /
Wikimedia Commons

p. 87 Pieter Bruegel the Elder, *The Blind Leading
the Blind*, 1568. Oil on canvas, 86 × 154 cm.
National Museum of Capodimonte, Naples, Italy /
Wikimedia Commons

p. 89 Robert Dighton, *Life and Death Contrasted*,
1784. Etching and engraving with hand-colouring,
34.8 × 24.4 cm. The British Museum, London
© The Trustees of the British Museum

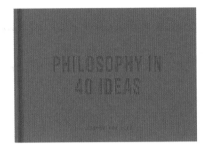

ISBN: 978-1-912891-47-4
£10.00 | $14.99

Philosophy in 40 Ideas
Lessons for life

A thought-provoking introduction to philosophy, spanning the history of thought in 40 key ideas.

Philosophy is a practical discipline committed to helping us live wiser and less sorrowful lives. This book draws together forty of the greatest ideas found in both Eastern and Western philosophy, spanning the history of thought from Socrates to the Buddha, Jean-Paul Sartre to Lao Tzu. We are reminded of the wit, humanity and relevance of the great thinkers, who have hugely helpful things to say to us about falling in love, making friends, finding serenity, discovering our purpose and enjoying what remains of our lives.

The word 'philosophy' hints to us why the subject matters. In Ancient Greek, *philo* (love) and *sophia* (wisdom) indicate that philosophy is quite literally a discipline for those who 'love wisdom'. Here are its most essential ideas rescued, highlighted and inspiringly presented so they can help where they are most needed: in our daily lives.

Art Against Despair
Pictures to restore hope

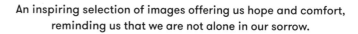

An inspiring selection of images offering us hope and comfort, reminding us that we are not alone in our sorrow.

One of the most unexpectedly useful things we can do when we're feeling glum or out of sorts is to look at pictures. The best works of art can lift our spirits, remind us of what we love and return perspective to our situation. A few moments in front of the right picture can rescue us.

This is a collection of the world's most consoling and uplifting images, accompanied by small essays that talk about the works in a way that offers us comfort and inspiration. The images in the book range wildly across time and space: from ancient to modern, east to west, north to south, taking in photography, painting, abstract and figurative art. All the images have been carefully chosen to help us with a particular problem we might face: a broken heart, a difficulty at work, the meanness of others, the challenges of family and friends ... We're invited to look at art with unusual depth to find our way towards hope and courage.

This is a portable museum dedicated to beauty and consolation, a unique book about art that is also about psychology and healing: a true piece of art therapy.

ISBN: 978-1-912891-90-0
£22.00| $32.99

The School of Life publishes a range of books on essential topics in psychological and emotional life, including relationships, parenting, friendship, careers and fulfilment. The aim is always to help us to understand ourselves better – and thereby to grow calmer, less confused and more purposeful. Discover our full range of titles, including books for children, here:

www.theschooloflife.com/books

The School of Life also offers a comprehensive therapy service, which complements, and draws upon, our published works:

www.theschooloflife.com/therapy

THESCHOOLOFLIFE.COM